Cross a Parted Sea

Books by Sam Cornish

Folks Like Me *(Poetry)*
Your Hand in Mine *(Children)*
Generations *(Poetry)*
Grandmother's Pictures *(Children)*
Sam's World *(Poetry)*
Songs of Jubilee *(Poetry)*
1935 *(Memoir)*

Cross a Parted Sea

Poems by Sam Cornish

Z
ZOLAND BOOKS
Cambridge, Massachusetts

First edition published in 1996 by
Zoland Books, Inc.
384 Huron Avenue
Cambridge, Massachusetts 02138

Copyright © 1996 by Sam Cornish

"Green Spring" was previously published in *Afro-American Alphabet* (St. Lawrence Press). "Cross a Parted Sea" and "Elegy for my Father 1945" were previously published in *Grand Street*. "The Beating" was previously published in *The Lowell Pearl*. "The Cross" and "The South Was Waiting in Baltimore" were previously published in *1935* (Ploughshares Books). "A River the World Knows" and "My Lord What a Mourning" were previously published in *Muddy River Review*. "Uncles" and "The Death of Martin Luther King, Jr." were previously published in *Compost*. "Death of Dr. King" was previously published in *Generations* (Beacon Press).

The Sterling Brown quotation is from *The Collected Poems of Sterling Brown*, selected by Michael S. Harper (HarperCollins, Inc., 1980). The quotation from the Negro Spiritual is also referenced in James Baldwin's *The Fire Next Time*.

All rights reserved. No part of this book may be used or reproduced in any manner whatsoever without written permission, except in the case of brief quotations embodied in critical articles or reviews.

Cover painting by Norman Lewis
Musicians, ca. 1930
All rights reserved

FIRST EDITION

Book design by Lori K. Pease
Printed in the United States of America

02 01 00 99 98 97 96   8 7 6 5 4 3 2 1

This book is printed on acid-free paper, and its binding materials have been chosen for strength and durability.

Library of Congress Cataloging-in-Publication Data
Cornish, Sam.
Cross a parted sea : poems / by Sam Cornish. --1st ed.
p.   cm.
ISBN 0-944072-71-2   (acid-free paper)
PS3553.068C76   1996
811' .54--dc20   96-16397
                                              CIP

To Harry Wells & Michael Mayreis

*This is the Lord's doing,
and it is marvelous in our eyes.*

Matthew 21:42

Contents

Mason-Dixon Line

Porter 13
Love Song of a Red Cap 14
Jack Rabbit in the Black Belt 15
Woke Up When Living Here Was Like Being in the County Jail 16
Alabama 17
American Earth 18
A Bed of the Ground 19
My Soul Died with America 20
Of Dusk and Valor Dunbar Sang 21
Soldiers' Elegies 22
Italian Elegies 23
Love Letters 24
To Cross the Parted Sea 25
America Knocks But Once 26
In the Company of Men America Knocks Upon the Door 27
I Walk Alone 28
Dog Town Slim 29
Buffalo Soldiers 31
Green Spring 32
Booker 33
A Clear and Present Danger 34
Something Terrible Something 36
Uncle 37
Neckbone 38
Sucked His Dick Cut His Throat 39
Sweetman 40
Mississippi on the Doorstep 41
Brotherman 42
The Royal Sassy Mouth 43
Jackie Robinson 45
Trouble in July 46
Niggers 47
Blues 48
Josh White 49

Brother Never Take Your Troubles Home Like a Mule Kicking   *50*
Hangover   *51*
Oh...So Good   *52*
Cold Cold Ground   *53*
All Through the Night   *54*
Cross a Parted Sea   *55*
Good Jelly Gives New Meaning to Mercy   *56*
Pastry   *57*
Go Tell It on the Mountain   *58*
My Father's House   *59*
Work to be Done   *60*
Men of the Farm Men of the Land   *61*
Omaha   *62*
Take Me There   *63*
Poor White   *64*
Log Cabin Negro   *65*
The American Dream of Jesse Owens   *66*
Langston Variations 1955   *67*
Foot in the Dark   *68*
Aunt Harriet   *69*
   1. *More Than They Do*
   2. *The Man with the Gate Mouth*
   3. *Weary Comes Softly and Low*
   4. *Little Boy Leaves Home*
What Work Often Is   *72*
Pitcher of Lemonade   *73*
For A Negro Lady of the Evening and Weekend   *74*
Brown Bomber   *75*
Elvis   *76*
Only the White Man Sings   *77*
Elegy for My Father 1945   *78*
Post War   *79*
Negro Me   *80*
The Song in the World is a Sharecropper's   *81*
Home of the Brave   *82*
The Beating   *83*

The Cross

Fannie Lou Hamer   *87*
   1. *Fannie*
   2. *Fannie Lou Sat Down at a Southern
      Lunch Counter in 1962*
   3. *Lilies of the Field*
The Cross   *90*
Man Called the River   *91*
My Banjo   *92*
More than Mississippi Allows   *93*
The Vertical Negro at a Woolworth's Lunch Counter   *94*
Lunch   *95*
Richard from Mississippi the South Has a Foot Up Your Ass   *96*
One Hundred Million Black Voices   *97*
Brother of the Streets   *99*
Lunch Counter   *100*
Life Was Poor   *101*
A River the World Knows   *102*
My Lord What A Mourning   *103*
The Pews on Sunday   *104*
Uncles   *105*
Negro Poet   *108*
The South Was Waiting in Baltimore   *109*
Tired From Walking But Not Tired Enough   *112*
That Kind of Man   *113*
The Death of Martin Luther King, Jr.   *114*
Cold Dead Fingers   *115*
Consider This Negro Woman   *117*
Migrant   *118*
Black English   *119*
1968   *120*
Death of Dr. King   *121*
Chocolate   *122*
Brother Poet   *123*
Bus Boycott   *124*
Catherine   *125*
Boogie Woogie   *126*

Mason-Dixon Line

These know fear; for all their singing.

Sterling A. Brown
Children of the Mississippi

Porter

Pullman porters all
look the same (black & simple)
        the name
is George

Lincoln freed
     the Negro
George Pullman put
       them
   to work

   on
   hotels on
wheels the Pullman
cars   Negroes
      working
      on the railroad   instead
of   the   kitchen
the fields   Pullman   from the south
and across the country
Negroes working boogie

woogie
balling   the jack
boot black
bellhop   busboy
Lincoln was the Negro's
friend   George Pullman put
them (to work) on the railroad
walking the dog
balling the jack

Love Song of a Red Cap

a country boy
livin' in the city
workin' the rails

I think o'
you
honey
I's hurtin'
fa' away
from home
(a dream of whippo-
will)
a thought
of you
my dusky
lady

your light
brown eyes

Befo' I's put
my red cap
on

Jack Rabbit in the Black Belt

this
hillside of Negroes
tilling   the land
brown-
faced men   crazy Nigger
teeth almost gone:
sharecroppers
uncles
brothers of
the soil
sons of Ham
of Br'er Fox
& Jack Rabbit
in the black belt

Woke Up When Living Here Was Like Being in the County Jail

A new day
Just begun
have mercy lord
A new day

Alabama

My   war is
    white
thugs:

the enemy
    the Cracker down
the street
    the Poles
    the Bohemian
    the German

the women
    wife
    and mother grandmother
    fair Negro women
    brown skin
    women
    lady-like and full of grace

American Earth

upon hearing of the rape
of the Scottsboro women

dead Nigger is a word
named Scottsboro

send the children
out of the room

lock up
the women
and throw
away the key

close your ears
woman

like men lightning
in their fingers
whiskey cheap
in the throat
tell me how
this train is going on
south where Dunbar
wrote 'the corn
pone's hot'
and the breeze
like the Negro and his
master is sighing

A Bed of the Ground

Men who understand sheep and cows
on beans & salt pork these men
who cook for themselves (what
ever else are they for)
can be weary of women
men who understand sheep and cows
make a bed of the ground
and call it home

My Soul Died with America

my soul
died   with America
was found again in Scottsboro
how long since the train
to Scottsboro rode the rails
like a hobo with his life in the sack
feet on the road   I   was a
Scottsboro traveling man
one of every five
     white women
cried Scottsboro

to the Negro people writes
the Communist party
"SCOTTSBORO THE SHAME OF A NATION
IS A BLACK MAN" all boys
ain't never going to be…
men Scottsboro are born
to the rope and the road

misery boys on the road
heading South
     night in the freight cars
from town to town the word

spread like those Negro
men the legs of white
women   saying
things   not fit
to print

Of Dusk and Valor Dunbar Sang

of colored soldiers
in the war
Negro troops troops
proudly
marching (like
a smile
going by)

as you put
your arm
around
my waist

for
my education
country and you
I proudly sweat
march and die

Soldiers' Elegies

eager to serve my country and be
    like my father   a soldier with my sword and cap
      my country to serve   my lady Miss Baker
      (like a country) to defend
      to love

the French before Josephine Baker
    searched   for tails "turn around Negro
    soldier boy" ran to hear Miss Baker sing
    she was for   the double V victory
    in war
      and at home

where the townspeople (white as Klansmen) fought the
    Negro (like Joe Louis smelling in the ring)
    with MPs the soldier and his gun

I saw her thirty years before she died
    remembered she had children of all races
    as her own

Italian Elegies

before I knew
           injustice
           so young I was
           concerned
           with myself

I heard of Sacco and Vanzetti
a folk song
about a robbery
two men died
in the chair   how the lights dim
a last wish
and supper
that turns to shit

           how the lights dim
before Sacco &
when Sacco and Vanzetti fried
        how the lights
           dimmed when Sacco and Vanzetti died

Love Letters

Ethel and Julius
    their faces so Jewish I swore I saw them
in the neighborhood   looking
at me   from *Life*
     Magazine   coming out
of the Treblinka and Buchenwald
of the world the faces
that made the jaw turn
to iron

I saw America
and her poor
all immigrants
and some   already
Native Sons

before I knew the Negro
I knew Sacco and Vanzetti
Ethel and Julius in letters
loving each other
and the world   as America
never loved me

To Cross the Parted Sea

Those Wonderful People in the Dark

Selma born
he knew the white
man's game
bribe Negroes
shoot Negroes
leave white
women alone
have a white
friend
in high places
play the white
man's game

America Knocks But Once

    when America
was hungry men
and closed factories
and roads
the sharecroppers
of Steinbeck's
Okies I
listened to the promises
of America
again and was never
for the Negro
worker
until the stock markets were down
and death worked
    like a mule
    hunger
    knocked on the doors crept
    underneath beds of the poor took her
    children what we owned   with the dust
    storms   and the whiskey   we
    were down like   America
    sitting   like a worry song
    a misery in the middle
    of the room at the foot
    of the bed

In the Company of Men
America Knocks Upon the Door

Joseph McCarthy (my savior) discovered
an America once lost
to me   a friend of Roy Cohn   my redeemer   Joseph
born in a clap-
board house   one of seven
children dreaming of America
like me   everyday   a Jew
living in a small town   a white (gay) and bright
American and everyday   with a father
that said   "steady work makes   a man"

I worked   at a desk
            a civil servant
            a father
            of three
            an American   until
the mailman
left a letter
from the government
            saying
that I was being
investigated

I Walk Alone

I became a Communist
        marched
for the Scottsboro boy
a Bolshevik
a Stalinist
but
then one day long
after Pearl Harbor I became
America again   and today
       jealous as only she (my
  country of Liberty) can be
America has knocked   upon my door

Dog Town Slim

For Nelson Nye

our grandfathers
were
hard as nigger
sweat
writers
that drank
the muddy
waters
of Mississippi
and the Congo
traveled
the world
in books
foot &
fist
through
Dunbar
Douglass
Johnson
and
Hughes
no Uncle Toms
but men
on Grand Street
or Lenox Avenue
left bank
or after hours
joint

upside
the heads

of Gentiles
or Crackers
or to Spain
fuck
fascism
and the Krauts

their   lives so crazy
that women
wrote
about them made
a music
called the blues

Buffalo Soldiers

For Willy Strode

we belong to   a generation
of waltz and parades of ceremony
as the Klan marched by
a world like theirs of Dunbar
and Washington   gallant men
of dusk and valor that Dunbar
sang

Green Spring

Coon songs
are like
green spring onions
a breath as lowly
as the poet's song
and brother rabbit's tale
Coon songs are a language
of rabbits and uncles
Negro boys and waiters
for whites deaf
to the sounds
of the field
and cabin folks

Booker

lay down
your bucket
where
you are   said
Booker T
and my father

my heart
is sinking
like the sun
did Booker
T lie
or think
our day
is almost
done

A Clear and Present Danger

my daddy is a Red
straight and tall
my daddy is a Negro
fuck (you)
USA & Dixie too
in the Mississippi

my color
is the worker's
blood
on Black Sunday

my country
'Tis Of Thee I Sing
when
the phone
is ringing
white men
in the hall
and J. Edgar Hoover
is listening

daddy
is a Red a Negro
has friends that sing
about a house
where men are white
and brown and of all
nations

daddy is a Red
standing straight
and tall

bowing his head saying "this
is America to me"

Something Terrible Something

judgment
is coming
the Black Maria
and the hearse
sometime after dusk
every Friday between
payday and church
judgment
is coming
is a song I sing
to myself
something terrible
something miserable
something
blue

Uncle

For Joel Chandler Harris

my old man colored man
dragging along in your coat
of many colors
like the leaves
of the forest this time
of the year pants patched against
the winter and briar patch
and weed and cold
don't you wish you were
a rabbit with long pants on
my old man colored man weary eyes a poppin'
with a story about a rabbit
drinking wine of peach and prune
and grape so good the taste
is struck
with lightnin' o' white and pure
like God's angry eyes and
the sour breath of Brother
Bear

Neckbone

Lover boy
Dancing man
have mercy
Mr
with your
flying
feet
black and tender

dancing
man
clean and sweet
negro
man

long and swinging
southern
man
face like a woman

a little
Jesus
tapping

have some
mercy please

Sucked His Dick Cut His Throat

poor man
women were
his crime
they kneeled
befo' his
sparklin'
teeth he
loved all
colors
but burns
his head
with Dixie
Peach

Sweetman

bitches knelt
before his
sparkling
teeth his
feet
was music
made just
for me

Mississippi on the Doorstep

came north
cross the line

saw Negroes on the street
walking (everywhere a Negro walking)
I learned to read
and still it seemed

freedom was a matter
of crossing the Mason-Dixon line

but no job no place
to live Mississippi you sit

on the doorstep   like a long lost
unwelcome cousin

Brotherman

For Herman Cornish

was never a boy
but always a son

his education
on the street
he
let his dukes
do his talking
      wore
mean threads
had a steady eye

seek and you
shall find
sd
brotherman quick
with the dukes
king of the avenue

The Royal Sassy Mouth

Ruth Brown
sings
about what
a girl
of color can do,

please understand
yellow
girl,
(You are
okay) the men
look and
grin,

light skin girl
straight hair
with your sweet
tight thing

and almost
white (not too black
but just right)

when Ruth Brown
does her
thing

they see me instead of
Lena

a sassy mouth
(no chicken shit
grin) & know what
a woman
of color
can do

Jackie Robinson

the uniform and ball
are white but Jackie is

New Jersey
Harlem separate drinking fountains
empty seats
at the back
of a southern bus
my world is on fire

my world is Sunday
and someday
Jackie in his uniform
white enough to be America

but now Jackie shines
like Louis Armstrong
like a preacher
in the church
he's the rock
the hidin' place
the uniform and the ball
and Jackie Robinson Negro

Trouble in July

Poor White Trash
does worse than drive
me crazy

Niggers

full of
cotton & jive
waking up
just glad
to be alive

Blues

(when your troubled women outlive you)

blue
my song (& his)
and color too
a poet from the fingers
(never did a lick o'
work)
his lips
made a sound
so deep & sadly blue
a no good
mean daddy
in the ground all
the dirt in his life
now shoveled in his face

Josh White

(Negro Never Take Your Trouble Home)

you ain't Ledbetter
Blind Lemon
with blues on your tongue

with breath like
a pig foot   Negro a silver spoon
in your mouth

& mouthin' a woman
drinking hard

someday
you 'ill wake up
all alone

you ain't Memphis
Slim

a blues man
guitar on yo' back

someday
you 'ill wake
up all alone

Brother Never Take Your Troubles Home Like a Mule Kicking

in 'fifty-three
a white man called
me boy

in the land
'¡f the bull whip
Nat Turner
Frederick Douglas
of John Henry

my anger drove
the ploughing
the hoeing
the planting I beat
the women folk now I
am a lonesome Negro
boy

brother
never take your trouble
home

Hangover

white boys call
me a bad Nigger   but
my woman   says I am
nothing
but a jackass
slopping chitterlin'
shucking and jiving
like the crabs
looking for something
to eat

Oh...So Good

old Negro man talkin' 'bout
yo' can feel in yo' walk
way down   in yo'   feet
when yo' talk

Cold Cold Ground

white woman standing
before the jury
dead nigger in the ground

All Through the Night

Walter White Nigger
on his mind a Negro   so
fair he can walk
away from a tree
where white folks gather
dressed for Sunday
and a hanging   Walter White so
fair   law in his mind
but a Nigger
in his heart
riding the Jim Crow Car
to the   other side
of the Mason-Dixon Line
Walter White moving through
the Southland
from place   to sorrowful place
Walter White   going
from tree to hanging tree

Cross a Parted Sea

in the Green
Pastures   God is a Negro
his cigars cost a dime

Heaven is a fish fry every day
where angels (wings pinned to
their white robes) are singing

and even in heaven the catfish
bite & drinking peach wine
is the only sin my father knows

my mother is dusting the lord's
wings sweeping heaven's floor
the little ones

eat too much watermelon
and they sing (all heaven
does) the spirituals before

there was a south a bondage
and the children
of Israel crossed a parted sea

Good Jelly Gives New Meaning to Mercy

it is jelly roll
when he thinks

of takin' a train
headin' back

for the lowlands
to New Orleans with it's

fancy (like diamond
rings) women

homemade jelly
good jelly giving

new meaning to mercy

Pastry

he thinks of home sweet
jelly hot jelly   Lawd

mercy jelly jelly my
jelly roll nice and tight

jelly jelly jelly roll
will make everything all right

my old man works hard
sunrise to night give

him jelly jelly jelly
it rolls his eyes make

them shine like his teeth
when he smiles

white
and full they shine
till his heart is warm

and full with the sweetness
of my jelly jelly roll

Go Tell It on the Mountain

on my knees I found God
in the air with a mighty
sword on the threshing
floor wrestling
with James Baldwin

on the street young and
wild without a dime hanging
out needle dangling from
my arm saying pussy
for sale in a parked car
I found God opening
his overcoat one button
at a time

in the alley
ways in the long dark
rows of adult movie
theaters a newspaper
spread over his lap
I found God
just doing his job

My Father's House

when my father
whipped me
with his strap
like a master
his humble
slave
beat me
with his fist
like his woman
when she was out
of line
he found God
as my blood filled
my shoes when he
brought me crying
and bleeding
to Jesus he saw Elvis
sweetly
singing
with his hips

Work to be Done

on the land we made
what city Negroes buy
no use
going to Detroit
the promised land
my father slaughtered
hogs worth more
than   dollar bills
my father worked till
he can't work no more
this ain't starvation
farm working long days
I hated that man his ornery ways
but there was no time
for southern blues
there was a rising sun
and work to be done

Men of the Farm Men of the Land

men on the farm
mean talking men
drinking good
time men like my
father in church
on Sunday work all
day getting the
land piece by piece
but   day by day
in the city
the rent man
knocks in the country
we live on the
land we slaughter
our hogs make
the bread plant the corn
men of the
farm men
of the land

Omaha

from the Indians its name
then the Irish Russians and Germans
came
my brother left
Omaha to be
a Bell Hop a Bus Boy (thank you George
Pullman for nothing) came home
with a dollar for my mother a dime
for sister and me (lots of money then)
he came home a friend   singing
Ma Rainey songs

Take Me There

Mississippi river   old time
religion   take me there   by the big muddy (over
     the Missouri   let me go   into freedom land)
     where   Jehovah speaks (and the bush burns
and the mountain speaks in the dreadful
darkness)
     near the stockyards
     "come home   come home"
     take me there
     Jesus is calling
     "come home   come home"

     take me there

Poor White

poor
white
why
did
life
treat
you so
so
low

them
democrats
don't know
poor

white
from
wrong

Log Cabin Negro

For Richard

work &
the bottle
the women   kill
you little   by little

your darkness   shines
like a silk shirt in the
the cotton fields

where I was a boy
a log cabin Negro always
            on the move
in the black belt

The American Dream of Jesse Owens

Jesse Owens ran with America
in his heart believed my country
"'tis of thee" (& me) in his legs he
had the strength to make America
be said Jesse "America" for
a Negro boy in all our cities
on a northern city street
on a southern road running
running running faster than
me because he (will) believe
in the American dream
of Jesse Owens

Langston Variations 1955

America is Good An Apple Pie
and maybe Emmett Till
in the small Negro pages of *Jet*
magazine in my soul where Words are fine
clothes for the Negro to die in

Foot in the Dark

one foot in the dark standing
in the doorway body full of potatoes
suitcase of blouses dress and pants
pants high above her ankles she
prepares to leave I had a caddlac
once she says and steps off
into the night

Aunt Harriet

1. More Than They Do

Aunt Harriet shares black
eyed peas   hog meat
her food is soul food
Aunt Harriet an old
woman talks and shares
her life full of
the Lord and memories
of slavery when white folks
saw as far they do now
and that is (she says)
more than they do   today
my aunt eats her black
eyed peas wipes her plate
with a piece of pone

2. The Man with the Gate Mouth

my aunt is waiting
for her daughter to come
home from the dance
from the high steppin'
the jazz band the crooked
leg man cabaret man
with the trumpet black man
with the gate mouth and horn
sweet man playin' the drums

on Sunday the Lord's day
jazz man slipping the devil

3. *Weary Comes Softly and Low*

my aunt has tended the sick
reaching to the old
like Jesus
she's stood before the old
darkness
death looming large
coming for the
aging old sister
& those who have slaved
long in king cotton's
land in debt and baggin'
cotton that ornery crop
my aunt a black woman
has stood her ground

4. *Little Boy Leaves Home*

now my aunt waits
with the horse whip
at her feet
for beating the devil
that's sinnin' &

dancin' in the long
legs of her muleheaded
traveling son
in his silk
shirt
& sinning ways
her los' boy
her no good son

What Work Often Is

no life for a man
working all day
legs apart
driving steel
laying more track
than any man
no wonder
his back is broke
sleepin'
in a boxcar is
no life for a man

Pitcher of Lemonade

St. Louis child black
face shining like sunflowers
and daffodils laughing on the fence

white man's child you are a pitcher
of lemonade golden child
his eyes are blue   but still
a nigger the lord will provide

little brown boy
grandmother favorite child

For A Negro Lady
of the Evening and Weekend

good pussy   day red
soil keep
her warm   lord may
                              her kale
and collards pot liquor
taste like white
                      lightning
till judgment

Master   slaughter for her
the best of the hog
somethin' better than the chitterlings
stinkin' up the ground

preacher everybody's got a soul
even you pray for
                 my Negro Lady
                 of the evening and weekend
till judgment
then
                 then let there be
                 plenty of smokes
and days of Ma Rainey
singing just
for you   my dark Negro
lady of evening and weekends

Brown Bomber

fist: Joe Louis The Brown
Bomber in the ring was the Negro
people   sweating and fighting
in the corner store   our small
rooms the pulpit resting
on the marble steps Joe Louis
fighting   from radio to radio

Elvis

his thing is singing
like a black
smoked down rhythm
and blues   white
boy the preacher
trembles   "that boy
is the devil sounding
like a laughing crazy jiving
nigger"

Only the White Man Sings

rain   falls
so hard
      in the Mississippi
      night the bodies
      hang   for days
      the crosses burn
      only the white man
      sings O carry me
            back

Elegy for My Father 1945

A Soldier Home   a southern boy
in the army   whiskey   never left
my side and when I played
my guitar   the south   spoke
my mind   now   with my duffel bag upon
my back uniform   still   on campaign ribbons
     on my chest
Captain bars
bright across my shoulders
I came home   south   (O where
the land   so beautiful
is a sorrowful one)
of shanty towns
Nigger Towns
Coal Towns
windows   stuffed
with   cardboard
& me   a southern
poor Negro   (church of God
in me prophecies of the nigger)

mad as the once angry Mississippi I thought
of (you) my father   working for five dollars
a day southern poor (long day poor
father)
now home I bring (to you and the south)
the   war
and cast
down my bucket
father
where you are

Post War

Where you are
(in the hands of Booker T)
        I cast down my
        bucket   &
        go south to sorrow where
The Negro walks
go   down   go south   way down
(no melting
pot   here in Dixie)
in the street   the white
man strolls   along the walk

Negro.Me

My Wheels & Old(s)mobile is like home
to me   driving my   car is a holiday
my wheels shines like   Satchmo &
the sun   but is darker   and more
like home & O' black   but
friendly Negro   me

The Song in the World is a Sharecropper's

Song traveling south   the song
in the world is a sharecropper   life's jealous hearted
song   of Tuskogee and Booker T
the separation and equality
like the five fingers   a gesture to illustrate and free
the Negro people
if Booker had looked   the palm of the   hand is pink
close to the skin   of whites of slave masters
and Klansman the hand that works that suffers
that grips and pulls and gestures is black
darker than the skin of Booker T and
some say   his intentions

Home of the Brave

Coming home I thought
my homeland   is not fabled Africa
or France   left bank of black
intellectuals and Jazzmen   reading the *New
York Times* drinking America getting drunk
on America
coming home   I know that history
is not a slave journal a runaway's flight
from the south
But Bessie Smith
and the urban blues
of my father
&   his world

The Beating

my mother's back or the abolitionist
tale. My mother's back is bleeding

like the avenues and streets
of American cities   is dark
& red like   barbecue

The Cross

*God gave Noah the rainbow sign
No more water, the fire next time!*

Negro Spiritual

Fannie Lou Hamer

1. *Fannie*

I am Fannie Lou small
Negro woman Lord's Woman
now Mr. Hamer's Woman
Southern woman not Stokeley rooting
out the Honky setting city
blocks afire Malcolm finding
in the blackness of his soul
his God nor King Minister's boy
college mind and manners
with a mighty tongue almost
a Moses but a Negro with God
in his throat anger in his heart
I am Fannie Lou and we are
climbing like the soldiers
of the cross upon Jacob's ladder
I am climbing   to say and sing
"this little light of mine"
even in the   southland
"I am going to let it shine"
I am marching at Selma bridge
and making freedom
one foot   in front
of the other   with faith
the Baptist   and the southern church

2. *Fannie Lou Sat Down
   At a Southern Lunch
   Counter in 1962*

Miss Hamer
sometimes just standing
up to sit down   America
crucified my lord

the hammer Miss Hamer rang
through the South & America
the land of Langston Hughes

and me Ms. Hamer how beautiful
you are just standing
then sitting down

3. *Lilies of the Field*

do not feed the lilies
of the field   they will grow
big and full   of starch
hungry southern and afraid

workin' mouth   chewin' starch
Fannie Lou Hamer sang
this little light a black
woman   givin' money livin'
with hunger Talkin' about

freedom

Fannie Lou
Hammer sweet southern
and Mississippi
through and through

on the side
street the back   roads marchin'
with King gettin' out the vote
Fannie Lou Hamer knockin'

on freedom's door sang "this little
light of mine I am going
to let it shine"

The Cross

The river is the Mississippi and the voices are those of Negroes. The songs of work and sorrow from the field are older than the Africa they never understood, the history in the books they cannot read, the history told in the shotgun houses, the wood stove. The river is the stuff of men and women weighed with anchor and anvil, battered beyond recognition, the river is more than Emmett Till, it is the people, it is the 1950s. Sometime you will hear of the stillborn Fifties, Happy Days, Innocent Times, about the benevolence of the era in which nothing happened. The Eisenhower years of barbecue and cocktail hours, duck tails for whites and konks for Negroes: greased hair, fried hair, black and shining like the sun. The sweat that shines on road gangs that sing as they pound and cry "Hey!" like Paul Robeson. Hammer black sweat, work and life. Black song is the river Mississippi, the river of Emmett Till The Fifties.

Man Called the River

Deep and ankle
bound
the Negro has
his
place
on the tree
deep
in this beautiful
river
chain and ankles
bound

My Banjo

talking
a music called
Claude McKay
if we must die
it should
be straight
up
the blues
of Crackers up-
side
the heads   of Gentiles
on the highway
    my   banjo
talking
like Baraka
dark prince
of poetry

More than Mississippi Allows

James Meredith bold and careless
black
was an education
about Mississippi southern
white Mississippi
shot bloody   James
Meredith
is a photograph
in *Jet* magazine
bleeding
on network news
The Afro-American
newspapers
James Meredith Nigger

The Vertical Negro At a Woolworth's Lunch Counter

in   some dark
Mississippi

what a shame
is America
to be
and salute
standing up

thought the
vertical Negro
sitting
down American

Lunch

at first we thought
America sat with us

waiting
for a cup of coffee

America with a fresh
& washed face

polite
patient America
churchgoing America

saying no more
take-out
have a seat

sit down
(Langston's darker
brother you
waited so long)

Richard from Mississippi The South Has a Foot Up Your Ass

nigger soot between his teeth   soot
in the cracks   of his skin   train
dust   in his hair black everywhere
in the shacks   between the floorboards

Richard   came one step   ahead
of the rope Richard Wright from
the South   the crazy brutal white
South (with a fist   in his mouth a rope
around his neck) many thousands gone
in the deep up from the blues
and sorrow songs Richard writing
in the dark

One Hundred Million Black Voices

in America everywhere
we walk we are
Negroes
our feet are
weapons our
words are the spirituals
we sing
our hearts thumpin'
the blues

in America everywhere
on death row we are
Emmett Till Medgar
Evers
the Strange Fruit
that Billie sings

about in white
night clubs
on the other
side of town

the meanest part
of town
where we hustle
before
the sun sets

and night falls

like a hammer
& what you see
is a man like the
devils Malcolm knows

Brother of the Streets

children
this is the blood
the other men named Uncle Remus
and sometimes Boy
and always brother
men of
mysterious deaths
sudden deaths
brothers of the streets
the poetry
and high-five
like old gods
from the mother country
strange and unknown country
of common history
origin
and many languages
and strange tongues
men who sacrificed
the Korean War
Detroit Riot
Harlem Riot
the Mississippi River
who found the soul of Africa in zoot suits
the songs hip from the street corners
the dusk in the voice of Billie Holiday song
for these brothers

Lunch Counter

we had lunch that day
all over America but the South
spit   poured hot
coffee   on my head

said go back to the jungle
hide in the trees   but we sat
those of us   who pledged the flag
the country   each morning

wore the uniform of the army the navy
and marines but   fought WW II
in the officers mess in Europe and Japan
washed the shirts   of the men
who dropped the bomb of a thousand suns

Life Was Poor

the people of Money, Mississippi
are good people   I sweep
their floors and wash
their children   they sing
the praises
of the lord and keep
his world and his word
the people of Money,
Mississippi White
people never had
any trouble life was
poor people   black
people domestic workers
school teachers   share
croppers Eisenhower
in the White House   separate
bathrooms   separate schools and
churches and the back
of the bus and there
were colored
water fountains

A River the World Knows

I knew the boy
I saw the flat nose
those thick lips and dark skin
so black for a northern boy
and
now darker 'cause of the sun
and deep South
and then I saw his ring
the boy's ring and
I knew that was my nephew
pulled from the river like so
many others thrown into the river
and now dead
for the Negro to see

My Lord What A Mourning

people went into their pockets
for his mother   gathered
their pennies   dressed
in their Sunday clothes
my mother washed my shirt,
and ironed my pants shined my
shoes with liquid wax
and we went
to church   we stood in line
to see the corpse of Emmett Till

The Pews on Sunday

"I have a dream," said
Martin Luther King Jr. White
people
had a nightmare,
looking at America,
beaten, and
exploding (like a raisin
in a Langston Hughes
poem) White America
was a dream burning in the streets
in Watts Chicago the smoke
over New Jersey over the shanties
the tenements
the pews on Sunday
morning

Uncles

For Herbert and Eddie

Lord take away
the weather in his bones so
all of them teeth can make a smile
he is a Baptist and can almost
break your heart
in the living room at the kitchen table
life is hard and the living
is where he finds it
uncle has a spittoon and ash tray
has arms where I can hide and smile and cry
smokes a fine big cigar almost a father
(and to some he is) uncles brothers of mothers
and fathers and friend of mine uncles black
and brown (some are yeller) married to sisters
men of the family strong as a big coal truck
at ballgames and barber
shops work in factories, grocery stores and liquor
stores takes the elevator up faster
than young feet on the stair
uncle was a sharecropper   from Alabama Mississippi
Virginia Rising Sun Maryland has paychecks and
Superman comic books comes equipped
with walks (and hugs) thick pork chops from the butcher
shop and pints of Pikesville Whiskey for himself
and Kosher wine sweet for Grandmother
because it's Jewish is good
dark and thick Shapiro concord grape

Uncle carries a pistol
and his friends call him Jim
say he sings like the Inkspots
with their ringed fingers and deep
southern voices not wanting
to set the world on fire
he just makes a woman's heart
smoke (a little) and cuss
the winter and the lonely life
my uncle with a strap put the fear
of God into my behind and nasty mouth
because I talked back to my mother
his sister his friend
he teaches first grade
in summer softball
now rides the rails serving
sandwiches and coffee
and shines shoes so black
they shine and say sugar daddy
'cause he pays
the rent brings soul food on Sunday
and a dime for me
before dinner bowing his head to lead
the table in thanks
in Jesus name Amen
uncles smell of smoke
and soap and work dancing and laughing
away trouble uncles

voices (is a drum) like thunder
laughter like lightly falling rain
thick fingers
and hands like
hunks of meat they are
family
when the father is dead
or walked away
all the men we want our fathers to be
all the men (I hope) we are

Negro Poet

That's me
A Nigger that Poetry
instead of Lincoln set free
a poem a Negro poem
a criminal   white haired dirty old
man that's me   Georgia not Africa is in my
blood and I am looking for work
no gambling or nightlife   just
women yellow black red brown white
women & dope   poetry that 's me
a Nigger that poetry set free

The South Was Waiting in Baltimore

Ruth Brown
sent bad songs about her brown body but I
could see white boys hit the nigger streets
saw them running through the projects looking
for colored girls the Fifties were marching
integrating schools
young Richard Nixon
barbers standing
in the doors of their
shops saying
shame shame
at the sight
of my hair
Negro men
scratched their heads
burned their hair
to make it
good
like Nat
King Cole
Emmett Till died
in Mississippi his
picture in *Jet*
magazine
his death a word on the streets I never
went to Mississippi
during the bus boycotts
nor sat in
for civil rights
and hamburgers

I was poor even
then my shoes were holes
held together
by threats & good luck but I read Camus
& listened to Martin
Luther King
the Muslims
in the temple
selling
bean pie
& promising the death
of white devils
the white
man
that never came
in my room
the students
freaked I read
about Algeria &
found James Baldwin
disturbing

some of my friends
made jokes
about Mississippi
I never rode
the Freedom Bus
but I
walked the streets

of Baltimore
visited Little Italy
the Polish
neighborhoods
near the waterfronts
you did not
have to travel
to the Southern
states
it was waiting
in Baltimore

Tired From Walking But Not Tired Enough

they bombed Dr. King's house and we kept on a coming
like Sterling Brown's men put Miss Parks in handcuffs
a nice respectable woman in jail and we started walking
kept on walking till our feet gave way
but we walked and the church was on fire
we were alive as the songs no longer sorrow
but the word that kept us going through the woods
following (once) The North Star kept on walking
in all kinds of shoes tired feet flat feet bad
feet feet that shouted when they sink into warm
water brought from the stove and poured into
a wash basin but at church we were tired
from walking but not tired enough to clap
hands and sing leaning on the everlasting arm

That Kind of Man

when I heard the boycott
was over could not
keep from crying
should have sung a hymn
but I ain't that kind
of man

The Death of Martin Luther King, Jr.

when the marching done Martin comes home
(long gone) in a mule-drawn cart
the students go (freedom summer o'er
some have   overcome)   America
the 'fro and go north to cities where in red buildings
hip and finger poppin' burning with black   power   to
funerals
and   Africa   the CIA the FBI The Mod
Squad   to listen to Marvin Gaye   smoke grass
cuttin' their   'fro's wearin' Super Fly shoes movin'
up up with George Jefferson running
like Sweet Sweetback   heels and shoe leather
smoking roaches runnin' like an old runaway
Ankle bracelet on the right leg   one eye gone
deep scar   on the left branded Black

Cold Dead Fingers

Imagine
Black Panther
Huey P. Newton
with a rifle
in one hand
a spear
in his fist

some brother
this Huey P.
solid and sharp
with a jungle
on his head

that looks

like desperate
death instead
of wild
but combed hair

Black Panther
in a wicker chair
brother
Marxist
ex-convict
Huey
P. Newton

owned

that chair
found
in a photographer's
studio

Huey
P.
sitting proud
in Oakland California

Consider This Negro Woman

bag lady this Negro
woman   the black
hair   her worn
coat   consider
this   Negro wo-
man   in the city
while the middle
class ponders
its death
taxes parking
meters consider
this woman the clothes
she wears   her white
scarf flowing
a sudden gust of cold
wind smoke   that clings
to the sky and hovers   moves over
the city the harbor this woman

Migrant

everywhere and every
place
on the street
the unemployment
a second language
of unpaid rent
seven to a bed
eating & sleeping
in a single
room
eyeing hubcaps
studying siesta
at Taco Bell

Black English

English
is the language
America
land of Eastern Europe
Henry Ford (remember
him)

1968

To Sisters shooting our Brothers

sing America Black
people write   this
word Nigger   all Black people
write NIGGER   in your shit
Nigger. Nigger. Nigger. Nigger.
Nigger. Nigger. Nigger. That's right
A Mother   Fucking Nigger, a mean
Nigger that's me   Death is Black.
Woman,   it's my Sunday best
in the middle of the week

Death of Dr. King

we sit outside
the bars   the dime stores
everything is closed today

we are mourning
our hands filled with bricks
a brother is dead

my eyes are white and cold
water is in my hands

this is grief

Chocolate

color this man
sweet
as candy
'cause solid
black ain't worth
shit

Brother Poet

Thig brother
    with a strut shot down
    in his prime bad
    poet of the nasty streets
    poet
    called the living
    lips

Bus Boycott

we
came home
ready to fight
the waitress
the short-order cooks
the counters
and stools the brown bags
served at the take-
out window
came
to a black south
that said
no to Rosa
Parks whose feet
said Enough
enough

Catherine

        will keep
        her child
instead of kill (mommy
always wanted a grand
baby) lovely
Catherine wild and loving
woman
proper
in church (but

    turned her
    back

    on the good book)
    now's ironing clothes

    to please

    her man

    hustling (school I
    rather be
    dead)

she said

Boogie Woogie

when every bar
is downtown

& named The Bucket
of Blood

Dizzy
& Louis
cutting
up   girl   ain't you glad
you
are fine
& Brown

Sam Cornish teaches literature and minority studies at Emerson College in Boston. His last book of poetry, *Folks Like Me,* was published by Zoland Books in 1993.